We really do need
Each Other

We really do need Each Other

by
Reuben Welch

impact
books
Nashville, Tennessee

Contents

Dedication

To Mary Jo—
With whom for twenty-seven years
I have shared the joys of being together.
And I have learned the lesson that togetherness
means that we really do need each other.

Chapter One

A PLACE TO MEET

I myself am on my own journey.
I don't come to you out of a vacuum.
I'm in the process of my own pilgrimage.
And I know that you don't come out of a vacuum either—
that you are on your journey.
And what I believe with all my heart is that in
the grace and mercy of God,
our providential meeting together
can be God's time for some new and fresh thing.
I'm writing to you about the things that I believe
the most and the best in the whole world.
I want you to know I'm writing about some of the greatest
stuff in the whole world.
And if I knew anything better to write about
I would write about it.
I want to tell you that I believe what I am writing to you
and I'm concerned that you believe it.
But whether you do or not,
I want you to know that what I am writing to you
I really believe with all my heart.

What I am sharing with you is both old and new.
It is old in that it is the word of the Bible
and has been true for a long time.
It is new because the old truth
has met me in the context of my personal journey
and is changing my life.

For about a dozen years
I've been a teacher
at a Christian college in California—
for the last five, I've been a college chaplain.
I used to teach Greek—
please be impressed—
and every year we translated First John.
Whether or not it changed many students,
somewhere along the way
it began to change me
and I began to see words like life
and light
and love—
especially love.
And I began to feel John's concern
for the Christian fellowship,
and I began to understand his teaching
that in Christ we belong together
and we really do need each other.

Then I became chaplain of the college—
and the book came alive
as I experienced the living needs
of a living community
not too different
from the one John knew in Ephesus.
I discovered that you don't produce community
by bringing X number of warm bodies
together
and running them through registration.
What a surprise to learn that
compulsory chapel attendance
does not automatically make us
"one in the Spirit"
and "one in the Lord".

From the outside
                    it would seem that
        a Christian college campus would be
                    a sort of an anteroom to heaven—
                            all these students
                    in a similar age group
                    with similar religious backgrounds
                    and similar socio-economic status,
and interested in Christian higher education
                            and all wise—
                    especially the sophomores.
But I have found out,
            that in the midst of all these
                    likenesses and similarities,
there can be fragmentation
                    division,
                insecurity,
            and loneliness—

                    mostly
                    loneliness.
I also discovered that what John talked about was true,
    not only for some special group
        somewhere a long time ago—
    it is all about real needs
                of real people like you and me
and it is true for us right where we are.

                I remember when we got concerned at school
about the possibility of a campus becoming ingrown
            and out of touch with the real live world.
        So in an effort to overcome our ingrownness,
we began to have dialogues
                            on race relations,
                            war and peace,
                            Vietnam, the draft,
                            sociological problems,
                                    etc.

So we had our panels and dialogues
and special speakers
and exposed ourselves to the wide world
and somewhere along in the midst
of the whole business
one of our students
tried
to commit
suicide.
I will never recover from that shock.
But here we were—
do you know what we said?
"We are the protected, sheltered
sub-culture
out-of-touch.
We live in a little hothouse
and out there are the real problems
and the real issues of the world.
We cannot do this.
We must expose ourselves."
And somebody right in the midst of us was about to
die.
While we considered the *real* issues of life.

Now I've been thinking a lot about that
and that is why I believe all the issues of life
and death
are present between you and me.
Despair, loneliness, guilt, frustrations
disillusionment, hate, bitterness,
love—you name it.
You name a human emotion—
a human experience—
and it is here between you and me.
We need not talk about some other world.
So let's not think about "out there."
Let's think about "us"
and where we are
and what God wants to say to us now.

I hope you will forgive me
　　for being too autobiographical but
　　　　I'm writing about the changing things
　　that have been happening to me
since the truth of First John has confronted
　　　　the life situation in my world.
　　　　You will end up knowing me
　　　　　　better than I know you—
　　and I wish it didn't have to be that way.
Since I am a teacher,
　　　　　I am going to give you an assignment.
　　　　If I give you an assignment I'll feel at home
　　　　　　　and if you don't do it
　　　　　　I'll feel more at home than ever.
I would like for you to read First John
　　　two or three times
　　　　　as you read this book.
Let's just pause here for a moment now and pray as we go.

Lord, here's the Word before us.
　　　　　What do you want to say to us from It?
　　　　　What do you want to say to me?
　　　　　If we know our hearts
　　　we are not so much interested in what men
　　　　　　　can say,
but we really are interested in what You want to say
　　　　　　　today.

Father, talk to us
　　and say to us
　　　　what we need
　　　　　　to hear from the Word.
　　　　　　In Thy name
　　　　we pray—
　　　　Amen.

Chapter Two

JESUS BRINGS THE LIFE OF GOD

Who is this Person in our world?; No gap; It's Jesus and me; Me and my and my inner life; Images of oneness.

That which was from the beginning
which we have heard
which we have looked upon
                and touched with our hands
                        concerning the word of life—
the life was made manifest
                and we saw it
                and we testify to it
                and proclaim to you the eternal life
        which was with the Father
        and was made manifest to us—
                                that which
                        we have seen and heard
                        we proclaimed also to you
            so that you may have fellowship with us;
and our fellowship is with the Father and
                        with His Son Jesus Christ.
And we are writing this that our joy might be
                                complete.
                                (1 John 1:1-4)

In this first paragraph of First John
            some great realities emerge.
The New English Bible has put a title on First John—
        it is "Recall To Fundamentals"—
and in this first paragraph of chapter one
            two of them stand out—
            "manifested life"
                        and "fellowship."

The "manifested life" of God in Jesus constitutes,
or brings together,
a "fellowship" of those who share his life
in which is found
the fullness of joy.
Come to think of it,
that's what the first section of this book is about.
In case you don't read it all, you can at least
underline that last sentence.
It's going to take me awhile to write about it.

In terms of fundamentals
the first one is very clear—
God's life
is manifested to us in Jesus.
Is it really true that God's eternal life
has come into our world
at the level where it can be seen
and touched
and heard
and felt
and experienced
and known?
Is that really true?
Is it true that the eternal life of God
has entered into our human situation
fully
totally
utterly?

If it is,
it is the best word
that our earthbound, sinbound hearts have ever heard.
We all know the world has been touched by evil.
But we must also believe that it
has been touched by the life of God.
I really do believe this—
I really do.

God's eternal life has come to us
                              right where we are—
                    that's right where you are
                    and that's right where I am.
Did you know that where you are now,
          feeling what you are feeling now,
                    thinking what you are thinking now,
Jesus Christ brings to you the very life of God—
                    not by some magic stroke of omnipotence—
          but by himself entering into our humanity
bringing with him the very life of God.
                              God's life released
                                   in my world?
                                   Yes,
                                        Yes,
                                             Yes.

                              Sometimes at school
                              I have the "privilege"
of teaching an upper divisional general ed. course
          with the profound title of
"Great Movements and Ideas Of Christianity."
It's kind of a poor man's history of Christian thought—
          one quarter,
               thirty pages of outside reading,
                    and a 200-word term paper.
                    It's one of those kinda neat courses.
                              We talk about
                                   God, Man,
                                        the universe—
                    past, present, and future.
We pick up from the time of the early church
          some of the great ideas and movements
that have been involved in the Christian faith.

We start off with the early church fathers—

you know,
the disciples of the disciples of the disciples—
in the period of the church
when they hammered out the great creeds,
like the Nicene Creed
and the Chalcedonian Creed—
aren't you impressed that I know these?—
when they hammered out the great stuff
that finds its expression
in the Apostle's Creed
and in our creeds
that we hardly ever read
or think much about.

You may find this hard to believe
but sometimes, when I am haranguing the students
in a most exciting way
about these fantastically interesting subjects
I get a kind of a radar feed-back from out there
that carries with it the feeling of SO WHAT?
So we have to stop awhile
and talk about the SO WHAT.
I don't think we would express the Creeds
the same way they did
if we had to write them again,
but I believe this—
they were dealing with the real thing.

There are two fundamental issues
that the early church hassled with
as it formulated its creeds.

One was—
Is Jesus really
        God among us?
        Is it really God who
        meets us in Jesus?
        What about Jesus?
                        We would say
                          it this way—
      "Is He really divine?"
Of course, we say yes, but that is
             a fundamental question.
You see, here we are
        earthbound, sinbound—
      we know something of our own human existence—
Jesus comes into our world
      and all the creeds that ever were
        are the effort to explain this question:
           what's going on here with this person
                    in our world?
Is He in fact God among us?
                Is He almost God,
                  nearly God,
                    like God,
              something like God?
        Is He the finest flower that ever grew
        in the human garden?
        Is He the greatest person who ever lived
        or
        is He God
             who comes to us?
      The creeds say that it is indeed
             God's life that comes.
It isn't just my life magnified,
        or my life purified,
  but it is God's life
             come into my world.

The other issue with which they struggled is this—
Does the life that comes to us from God
really come all the way?
In common terms, the question is—
"Is Jesus really human?"
That's fundamental, isn't it?
Here we are—
earthbound, sinbound.
Is it God's life that comes?
Yes.

Does that life really come,
does it nearly come,
almost come,
or does Jesus enter
fully and totally into our human situation?

I think we believe in the humanity of Christ—
but not really.
I think you think
you believe in the humanity of Jesus—
but I don't think you really do.
And if we would talk about it awhile,
you'd get nervous.
I could write a long time about the divinity of Christ
and you might nod your head and
slowly go to sleep about it,
but when we begin to think about the real humanity
of Jesus

we get nervous—
we are afraid of it.
I don't know why.
Well yes, I guess I do.
We can safely think about the divinity,
but when we think about the humanity
that gets close to where we are
and then when we think about that
we get a little bit spooked.

I think we can put it this way—
                although I'm not sure the creed writers
                        would have said it this way—
        between Jesus and God
                    there is no gap.
            The other half of that is not so easy
                            for people like you and me—
        between Jesus and me
                    there is no gap.
                        Of course, we look up to Him,
but in a deep and wonderful sense—
        we don't look up to Him—
            we look straight across at Him.
                Not because we are exalted
but because He has come down all the way to meet us
flesh of our flesh
                    bone of our bone
                            humanity to humanity
                                eyeball to eyeball.

What good is it if Jesus comes to us
but He really doesn't come from God?
            And what good is it if He comes from God
                            but He doesn't really
                                come all the way?
            He is as much one with us
                    in our humanity,
        as He is one with the Father
                in His divinity.

Now when this begins to get hold of us
                we can begin to see that Jesus comes to us,
                not in the exaltation of our humanity,
                but in the depths of our human need.
Do you think we can believe that Jesus comes to us
                in our times of deepest need,
                        as we are at our worst?

What this means is
    that into your world
        your context
        your lifestyle—
            I mean just like it is,
            just exactly like it is—
    Jesus comes all the way
        and He brings with Him
        the very life of God.
And so there's the hope for my world
            and your world
      and our great big wide world.
If I could always believe it as much as I do
      when I am writing it,
and if you could believe it as much as you do
      when you're reading it,
what a wonderful difference it would make.
                He doesn't say
                "I'm up here.
                Reach up.
                Come up.
                Shape up.
                Get with it.
                Do right
and I'll meet you somewhere in between."
He comes from God—
        bringing God's life—
          "manifested life"—
               to where you are
                 as you are,
                what you are,
                    now.

The second of the great realities
about which John writes is "fellowship."
In that wonderful word "fellowship"
John includes the whole idea
of God's saving purposes
His salvation history
and redemptive deeds.
Let's look at the passage again.
The life was made manifest,
and we saw it,
and testify to it,
and proclaim to you the eternal life
which was with the Father
and was made manifest to us—
that which
we proclaim also to you
so that you may have fellowship with us.
(1 John 1:2,3)

Is he saying that all the reality
of God's manifested life—
that the great truth of the incarnation
is funneled down into fellowship?
Pre-cise-ly.
That's just exactly what he says.
I believe with all my heart
that the bringing of His life creates fellowship.
That which
we have seen and heard
we proclaim also to you
so that you may have fellowship with us;
and our fellowship is with the Father and
with His Son Jesus Christ.
(1 John 1:3)

Fellowship!
See—yours with us and
ours with Him
through His Son Jesus Christ.

Now let's think a little bit
                about that word "fellowship."
I have to tell you that I am at a place
                in my own journey where
                that word is very,
                                very important
        and I'm going to write about it longer
                                        than I should,
but not as long as I want to—by a long shot.
What an important word that is
        and I do speak to you out of the context
                of my own life.
                        You see, I have come to believe
                                with all my heart
                                that the life that Jesus brings
                                        is a shared life.
The life of God in the world
                does not have its meaning in isolated units,
                but in a fellowship of those
                        who share that life in Him.

The word "fellowship" in Greek is "koinonia."
                        You know, Sunday School
                                classes are named that.
                        It means to have a share
                                a sharing together
                                a common participation
                a partaking together
                a having in common.
                        Now as it is used in the New Testament
                                it is a distinctly Christian word.
It has other uses and meanings—
                        for instance,
        Peter and John had koinonia in the fishing business,
                        they had a shared partnership.
                What brought them together was their
                common sharing of the life of fishermen.

The point is—
Christians are not brought together
        because they like each other,
    but because they share a common life in Jesus
                            and are faced with the task
                    of learning how to love each other
                            as members of the family.
I'm sure you could not believe there is ever
            any tension in our home.
There are four of us who live there.
        We have three children—
                two at home.
        We don't live there
            at our house
        because we just met on the street one day
        and decided we liked each other
                            and decided
                    to take up living together.
We live together because we are a family,
            and sometimes in the midst of the strife
                    and tension and stress
        what holds us together
        is not the happy fellowship and congeniality
                but the fact that we are a family.
                    And because we are,
                we're faced with the continual task
                    of learning what love means.
What brings us together is not
        our mutualities and congenialities
                and common interests and hobbies.
                    It is not our mutual esteem
                        nor our happy hormones—
            it is our blood ties,
                    our common name
                and our common commitment—
    it's our parentage,
        and our heritage
            and our bloodline
                and our life.

And I think that is apt for the church.
So often we say
　　"You ought to come to our church—

　　　　　　　　　　　　you'd like us.

You'd like our preacher
　　you'd like our music
　　　　you'd like our youth program
　　　　　　you'd like our golden agers
　　　　　　　　our fifty-plusers—
　　　　　　　　　you'd like us.
　　　　　　　Come, please come
　　　　　　　　　do come
　　　　　　　　you'd like us."
And if they come—
　　and like us
　　then well and good.
　　But if they don't like us—
　　　　they spin off
　　　　and we say, "Oh, too bad.
They just never did seem to fit in, did they?"
But you see, the church
is not the society of the congenial—
　　　　it is a fellowship
　　　　　　based on common life in Jesus.
　　　　　　　　　It is the will of God
that the Christian life be lived in the context of a
　　fellowship of the shared life.
　　　　When I read that back it really
　　　　doesn't seem so profound—
but that really has been changing me.
　　　　　I am at a time of emphasis
　　　　　　upon the fact
　　　　　　that God has made us in such a way
　　　　　　that we really do
　　　　　　　need each other—
and maybe I am reacting against
　　what seems to me to be
an over-emphasis on individualism
　　in evangelical Christianity.

Some of us are so westernized
        and individualized
        and evangelicalized
                        that we have forgotten
                        how much we really
                        need each other.
I think people like you and me are grossly
                        over-individualized.
I think we have talked about personal salvation
                and individual salvation
                and "me" and "my"
                and "my inner life"
until we have almost isolated ourselves.
And so
we just get the idea that
    it's my life
  and God's life
            and you have your relationship to God
                and I have my relationship to God
            and of course we ought to
            be nice to each other
                        and love each other,
            but what really counts is
                    "my relationship to God."
                        We Christians act
                as though we are deep sea divers.
Here we are in the murky waters of sin—
  but we have the protection of the diving suit of God
                                    and
                    we have the lifeline
        that goes to the great white ship up above.
You have your life in Christ
                    and your lifeline
and I have my life in Christ
                    and my lifeline
                and here we are with all our lifelines
                            going up.

And we say to each other
  "How's your lifeline brother,
    you got any kinks?
      Get it straightened out,
        keep the oxygen going
          or the murky waters of sin
                will come rushing
                      in on you."
  We wave to each other
and write notes to each other
    and we bump each other around
    and we say to each other—
                "Get your lifeline
                        right."
                  But here I am
                  all by myself.
      Once in awhile someone gets the bends
      and we bump him up to the top
      or just cut him off
                and let him
                drown.
                That's not the way it is—
            because our life that we have with God
                is not just my life and His—
                        no way.
I know this vertical relationship is fundamental.
I know that what constitutes us a community
              is His life given.
    I'm not saying
        that our relationship to God
          is not personal and unique.
            I'm saying that we are over-
                    individualized.
      You know what I'm doing
      I'm over-exaggerating—
      but not very much.

The
vert-
ical
line
of
God-
ward
rela-
tion-
ship
and the horizontal line of human relationship
are not two lines but one line in a continuum.
It all belongs together.
I'm not talking about what ought to be
    or what would be nice if it were—
        I'm talking about God's reality
            about the way He has constituted
                the life we have with Him.
Our life with Him is tied to,
                is one with
                our life with our brothers
                        and sisters.
Like the old hymn says—
        "You can't have one without the other."

There are a couple of ideas
    going around in my mind here
            and one of them is this isolation thing—
            this over-individualization that we have.
When we feel like we are slipping spiritually
                or growing cold
                or indifferent
we have a tendency to withdraw and pray through
                or to get hold of God
                or get back to where we ought
                            to be
            so we will have something to give
                        to others—
                and that's false.

That separates the full and the empty
                    the haves and the have-nots—
            we are all have-nots,
            we are all emptys.
Somebody said, "Real witnessing is
            one beggar
            telling another beggar
                    where to get bread."
                            We are all beggars—
        we don't have anything but the life of Christ
and his life in us is not separate
                            from our life with
                                    each other.

And I think we are helped in this feeling of isolation
            by the songs that we sing.
                    I'm thinking of the old song,
            "On the Jericho Road,
                    there's room for just two
no more and no less
                    just Jesus and you."
                        And I remember the chorus—
            "Now it's just Jesus and me."
I live at school you know
        and I think the only time
            that song is appropriate
                is on a Friday night in the dorm
                    when everybody else
                        is on a date.
                    Then that's a good time to sing,
                "Jesus and me."
Here's another:
            "When I am burdened
                    or weary or sad
            Jesus is all I need"
or:
            "Are you weary,
                    are you heavy-hearted
            tell it to Jesus alone."

Of course there is truth in all these songs.
        Of course we believe in the total adequacy
                of Jesus Christ
                        to meet the total need of
                                the total person.
                But we must remember this also—
He saves in the context of the community of faith.
        It isn't "Jesus and me"
                it is "Jesus and we"
                        and on the Jericho Road
                                there is room for Jesus
                                and the whole redeemed
                                        community.
                        And if you are like me,
                                when you are
                        burdened and weary and sad
                        you need Jesus but you also need
                someone to be Jesus to you—
someone to bring His healing presence to you.
And sometimes the answer to your weariness
                        and heavy-heartedness
                        is not to "tell it to Jesus alone"
                        but to begin to share
                        and care with someone else.
You can get yourself in a little spiral of self-pity
and so you tell it to Jesus alone
                        and increase your self-pity
                        and your martyr complex.
                        "Lord, I'm so persecuted.
                        but Lord you understand."
                                Way to go.
            That's enough to bless this dying world, isn't it?
        Well, let's go on singing the good songs—
                        it's okay.
                They aren't true, but it's okay.
You see we really do need each other,
        not because of the inadequacies of God
        but because this is the way His grace works.

I suddenly remember a student at school
who just before he was to graduate
had to go into the hospital with cancer—
                                    and he died.
                        He was twenty-two,
            and he was a ministerial student
and Frank Carver, head of our department, and I
                        were very close to him—
and we went out to see him and had long talks with him
                about life
                        and death
                                and God.
    He knew what was happening and he said,
                                "You know,
            I know that God has worked in the past
and I know that God will be with me
            when I cross the river.
        I know He will be there,
                it is those times in-between
                    that sometimes are rough."
Do you understand that?
Sure you do and so do I.
                    I know God has been with me,
            I know God will be with me in the crisis,
                        but here I am right now.
He said,
"I just wish I was conscious of His presence at all times,
                                    like now
                        when I need it."
And Frank said to him,
"You know,
        Jesus comes to you
            in the persons who come to you."
                            Now that is true.
                        Have you experienced that?
                            I have.
It is also true
            that people can bring the devil
                and sometimes we're more familiar
                        with that.

But once in awhile someone comes
                              and brings
                                        Jesus to me.
          God has made us this way.
          We really do need each other.

The point of the passage here, I think,
          is that Christians are to recognize this reality.
John was calling them back to the fundamentals
because the fellowship was being threatened,
as it still is.
                    How is it healed?
                              By coming back to
                              the great realities
                              that constitute what we are—
                              the life that we have
                              in Jesus is a shared life.
Early Christians were often together
          around those things
               which made them what they were.
               They often met together to express
                    their oneness in Christ—
                    around the teaching
                    around the Word
                    around the sacraments
               and around prayer.
They were being together as Christians
          not just Christians being together,
                              I think this is more
                              than playing with words.
                    There is a fundamental difference between
                              the fellowship of Christians
                    and Christian fellowship.
Too often we are together as Christians
                    doing the things we like to do together—
                         volley ball, parties, teas, leagues,
                              receptions and what-not.

Or we get together and talk about cars
and sports and babies and clothes
and weather and Sunday School attendance
    and we come away having talked
                and laughed
                and enjoyed ourselves;
                            but strangely
                        empty and lonely
                    and a little bit guilty.
It does not deepen
    the oneness of the fellowship
        to multiply such activities.
    These things do not express our oneness
        but the study of the Word does
                the sacraments do
                and prayer does.
We need to be together more
    doing the things that really give expression
        to the common life we share.

    You know the best symbol of all this—
        the Lord's Supper.
I have a mental image about the Lord's Supper.
        I see a table in the upper room—
Can you see it?
            Jesus is at the head of the table
            and the disciples around the sides.
    And then I see the wall open up
            and the table begins to lengthen—
                and it lengthens out through

                            the first century
                        and the second century
                and it comes all the way into our world
                            to where we are.
Jesus is at the head of the table
            and all the believers of all the ages
        are gathered at the table
            and we are one
                at one table
                    with the Lord.

What is it that makes us one?
We share that broken,
                    given life
and so we come
and we are one.

There is a beautiful phrase in Galatians 2:9
            that expresses this.
Paul and his company had gone out from Antioch
                        into the Gentile world
and the saints in Jerusalem were insecure
    because the "general board"
        hadn't approved it.
                    But they had gone out on their own
                    and they were coming back
                            somewhat anxiously
                    and the church gave them
                    "the right hand of fellowship."
It meant that across the prejudices
                across the hesitancies
                across the insecurities
                across the normal barriers
                    that would have separated them,
                        they reached out and said,
            "God bless you—
            here is my hand."
And I tell you this—
if somewhere in this world
        there are people who are sharing
                the life of Jesus together
                    and who are helping each other,
                    and suffering with each other,
                            that's my crowd.
                Those are the people—
            that is the community
of which my heart yearns to be a part.
And the name of it is the church
                    the body of Christ
                    the fellowship of believers.

Let's pray—
   Lord Jesus,
teach us to know
 that what makes us one
   is our oneness in the Lord.
And don't let us dilute
     or weaken it
     until we become
       a society of the congenial.
           We would be indeed
           the body of Christ.
Teach us to know
 how very much we need each other.
 Help us to learn how
 to be sensitive to each other
 and open and accepting of each other.
Thou who has brought the life of God to bring us
            together—
   may our fellowship be the fellowship
    of the Father
     the Son
      and the Holy Spirit.
         Amen.

Chapter Three

WALKING IN THE LIGHT OF GOD

God is a good person; Taking the roof off; To say the same; But if.

So Jesus brings the life of God into our world;
   He brings it all the way down
      to where we live.
The life He brings is a shared life,
                           a life that creates a fellowship.
I wish I hadn't already written about this
            because I could write about it
               and write about it
               and write about it.
But there's some more great stuff
               to be said
               about the quality of life
            within this fellowship.
            Now the question that arises is this:
What is to be the quality of life within this fellowship?
What kind of a life is it that is shared by those who are
                           partakers
                        of the life of Christ?

I have come to believe
      that the life we share together in Christ
      is to be a life of openness
               and honesty
               and confession before Him
               in deep recognition of our humanness
                           and weakness
                           and failure.

Let's begin here:

This is the message we have heard from Him
and proclaim to you
that God is light
and in Him
is no darkness at all.

(1 John 1:5)

I think that is a major premise.

I wish you could hang a big sign from the ceiling—
put it high enough
because we are going
to hang some little
signs beneath it—
hang it out in front of you
and print on it these words:

God is Light.

Every once in awhile you can look up from the book
and see it.

Don't take it down—
it needs to stay there.

It's the major premise
and everything else we are going to say
hangs on the hooks underneath.

That's where it begins,

God is Light.

And John adds this phrase—

and in Him is no darkness at all.

In the Greek language they don't mind double negatives.

We don't use them
but the Greeks did
and John did it on purpose for emphasis
and what he really meant is
that there is no darkness in God—
no, not at all,
no darkness . . . at all,
none,
no darkness,
never no how.

Let's think about that for a minute.
The idea of God being light
  is not unique to the Christian faith
    or to the Judeo-Christian tradition,
                    but in the Biblical context
    it has some specific meanings that
    are tremendously significant to us
    in relation to our life
    in the fellowship of believers.
One of them is—
    God is light . . .
      and you can trust Him.
God doesn't have any dark folds in His cloak.
      There is no deceit
            no caprice
            no trickery
            no hypocrisy
            no game-playing with God.
    He is light
      is true
      is pure—
  He is sincere.
      We don't use that word about God
      but He is sincere.
God is a person of integrity—utterly.
He is not hiding anything beneath the folds of His garment.
        He is open
          is light
          is true—
        He can be utterly trusted
        because He is light.
Now that doesn't say anything that you didn't know already;
but how often we think of God
  and talk about Him as though
  He were a hidden, deceitful God
    with things about Him that you can't really trust
    and you better be careful.
But I tell you God is not like that;
      God does not play games with us.

Can we believe in the basic integrity of God?
I've talked to people
   who talk about God as though when they prayed
                        they had to say it right
                        or He wouldn't answer.
                  Can you hear God saying,
      "I want to help but you aren't asking right,
               so there's nothing I can do."
And people who think you have to be careful
   what you tell God you won't do
      because sure as the world
         that's just what He'll make you do.
You know, don't tell God you won't go to the jungles
                        as a missionary—
      because He might be up there saying,
            "I heard that!
               And I've got news for you."
I've talked to people who talk
                  who think
                  who believe
                     that He says,
         "You think you know what I want you to do,
            but you wait ten years
            and when you are way out here
            I'm just going to cut you off."
Sometimes we get to feeling that way,
   as though we have to penetrate the mystery.
                  But God is light,
                  there is no darkness in Him.
                  He is not trying to trick you.
      We are not dealing with darkness—
      we are not dealing with subterfuge.
                        I think I spelled
                        that big word right!
            We are dealing with light.

Maybe I ought not to write about this
  but I think I will anyway.
We've all heard about the invisible deadline . . .
                    when you say no to God
                            and no to God
        there's an invisible deadline
                    and when you cross over,
                            you have had it.
And you don't ever know when you're crossing over
            so you'd better be careful.
                    That doesn't compute
                    in terms of
                    God is Light.
You know, here you are on the path of light
      and you come to the last no—
                        usually about the
                        fourteenth verse of
                        "Almost Persuaded"
                on the last night of fall revival
                        and you've had it.
As though God has drawn an invisible line across your path
    and when you cross it
      even though you don't know it
      you have had it.
We know it is dangerous for us to say no to God
        but He will not damn us
            for crossing an unknown line—
                because He is light.
Either that is true
                or it is not true.
    And if God is light
        in Him is no darkness.
If we are going to talk about shadows and darkness
    we're not talking about God
        we're talking about us
        and that is what the rest of the passage
                            is about.

That does not mean there is no mystery about God
                            and His providence—
                    He is God and we are human.
We are not "on top of" Him to understand His ways—
            you can't say I understand mathematics,
                                    English,
                                    and God.
But this we have got to know and believe—
                        He is a good person,
                        He is light,
                        and we can trust Him
                                totally.

Another Biblical meaning
    of the phrase "God is Light" is this:
                        God is light,
                        God shines,
                        light shines!
                        That's quite profound—
aren't you glad you read this book to find that out?
                Light shines!
                            He is open to us.
                            He reveals Himself.
The life of God comes to us
                as light that shines in Jesus.
The light of God
    which is beyond our comprehension
        is focused on us in Jesus—
        God shines toward us in Jesus.
                        In Him
        we see the brightness of God's glory,
            the expressed image of His person.

The pure,
  holy,
    God of integrity
        shines in the life of Jesus Christ.
            Jesus said,
              "I am the light of the world."
In the face of Jesus
  we behold the light of the glory of God.

But what about us?
Here we are in a fellowship
created by the given life of God
            who is light—
              but we are not light.
         He is light but we are not light.
Then what is to be the quality of our lives?
This seems to me
  to be the very issue
    faced in the scriptures that follow.
    Now what we want to do
          is to hang six smaller signs
          down below the big one—
       each of which begins with the word "if."
             They are couplets,
       and they are kind of opposites.
They go like this:
If we say
  we have fellowship with Him
  while we walk in darkness,
    we lie
      and do not live
        according to the truth . . .
              if we walk
              in the light
           as He is in the light
       we have fellowship with one another,
and the blood of Jesus his Son cleanses us from all sin.
               (1 John 1:6,7)

If we say
  we have no sin
  we deceive ourselves
    and the truth is not in us.

                 If we confess our sins,
                 He is faithful and just,
            and will forgive our sins
      and cleanse us from all unrighteousness.
                     (1 John 1:8,9)

If we say
  we have not sinned,
  we make him a liar
  and his word is not in us.

                If anyone does sin,
          we have an Advocate with the Father,
            Jesus Christ, the Righteous.
               (1 John 1:10, 2:1)

Notice that the first line of each couplet begins with,
                "If we say,"
each one is followed by words that indicate in some way
    a denial,
  or a rejection,
  or an ignoring of our humanness
           our guilt
           our weaknesses
           our failures and our sins.
                  "If we say,
                  if we say,
                  if we say"—
evidently somebody around Ephesus was saying.
             And John is saying,
                "No-no, no."
          Look up at the first one:

If we say
  we have fellowship with Him
    while we walk in darkness,
      we lie,
        and do not live
          according to the truth.

Look,
God is light
        and if we say we have fellowship with Him
while we are still walking in darkness,
                        that's not true,
                        that is a lie.

God is light—
we cannot say
we have fellowship with light
                        and walk in darkness,
                        no way.

That's probably what it says in the Greek—no way.
    What does that mean in plain English?
I think it means
    that the quality of our lives
        does make a difference—
            there is no way to say it doesn't matter.
            Don't get to thinking that cutting the corners
                        doesn't make any difference—
                        it does.

God is light—
    in Him is no darkness.
                        If you think a few shadows
                        now and then
                    don't make any difference—
                        that's a lie.

We have lots of ways
    to handle our failures.
        We can rationalize them
                define them,
                ignore them,
            or pretend they don't make any difference—
                        but that's not true.
            You can't write them off that way.

**God is light—
in Him is no darkness.**

Let's look at the second one:
If we say
 we have no sin
 we deceive ourselves
  and the truth is not in us.
We cannot say
 sin does not belong to us.
If we deny the reality of sin in our nature—
                    no-no, not me, not us—
if we deny our fundamental sinfulness,
we are only deceiving ourselves
 and turning away from the truth.

                    The truth is, you see
we are sinners
 born into the stream
  of a sinful humanity
   and there is no way to deny that
   and keep squared with the truth.

Here is the third one:
If we say
 we have not sinned
 we make Him a liar
  and His word is not in us.
                    We aren't supposed to cover up
                          hide or deny,
                      defend or define,
                       or pretend
                that our weakness or failure
                          and sin
                       didn't happen.
We cannot refuse to accept the reality
 of failure in the acts and attitudes
  of our lives.

I know a dear family,
　　and once in awhile
the father gets his feelings hurt
　　　　　　　　　　　　　or is disappointed,
　　　　　　　　　　　　　or misunderstood—
　　　　　　　　　　　　　and when that happens—
　　　　　　　　　　　　　he just clams up.
Now don't get nervous,
　I'm not talking about you—
　　I'm talking about the father.
　　　　　　　　　　　　He handled this by total withdrawal
　　　　　　　　　　　　　　from the flow of family life.
　　　　Oh, he said good morning
　　　　　　　　　pass the potatoes
　　　　　　　　　and thank you—
　　　　　　　　　but he really wasn't there.
And then everybody else
　　would start walking around softly—
　　　　"pussyfooting it" is the term, I think—
　　　　　　　　　　　trying not to upset Father
　　　　　　　　　　　and trying to keep peace.
I'm not talking about you, I'm really not.
　　　Father was miffed
　　　Mother got a migraine,
　　　and everyone was paying for it.
　　　But one fine day
　　　Father was alright again
　　　and everything was okay.
　　　　　　　　　　　　　He had some way
　　　　　　　　of communicating this to the family—
　　　　　　　　　some word,
　　　　　　　　　some gesture,
　　　　　　　　　some small gift or conversation
　　　　　　　　　　　　would signal the family
　　　　　　　　　　　that he was alright again
and life would come on back to "normal"
　　with never a word to indicate
　　　that anything had ever been other
　　　　than perfectly regular.

The migraine faded,
the tiptoeing ceased
all as though nothing
had ever been different
and the incident was never mentioned—
ever.
You understand that, don't you?
Here is this detour—
undiscussed
unconfessed
unshared
unrecognized
denied
"it didn't happen."
So life now is supposed to go on
until by and by
it would happen again.
And everybody was supposed to pretend
nothing was changed
nothing was different,
everything just like it was,
and God's word says—no.

He is light,
He is truth.

He does not play games with us
and we cannot play games with Him.

Then how are we to respond in terms of our weakness
and failure
and sin?
Perhaps we need a parenthesis here.
The word that is used in this passage
is the word "sin"
but it is the word "sin"
in the broadest sense,
of "missing the mark."
It's "harmartia."

Some groups use the word "sin,"
for anything short of the divine ideal,
whether it is a bad mood in the morning
or shooting your grandmother at night.
And some people
just don't use the word "sin" at all
in connection with Christian people in the church.
You say sin
and they
immediately think of the
bad guys on the outside.

Since it's not easy
to make all those fine distinctions
I would like to put it all together
and use the word "failure."
Maybe then, we won't be so tempted
to pass this section of First John
on to others who need it.
We "all" need it.

I don't think it is right
that there should be
any part of the Bible
about which we can say,
"Oh, I've already finished that exercise—
now let's go on to something else.
I've passed my exam on First John."
I have a feeling that all of the Bible
keeps speaking to all of us
all of the time
and since this passage has something
to say to us,
wherever we are on our spiritual journe
I'm trying to find a word
that isn't a "red flag" word.
If I would talk to you about "sin"
there would be a kind of a resistance,
but I believe we all know something
about the meaning of "failure"
in our Christian life.

Sometimes when I am speaking on this subject
I ask the question,
"Is there anybody here
that doesn't know anything about failure?
Would you please stand
and we will pray for you
and the other liars."
Alas, I alone am usually left standing.

John is not speaking
to any specific group in the church—
he is not distinguishing between the "carnal"
and the "spiritual."
He writes to the church and
to all those in its fellowship.
And through the passage
he speaks to us
who, on our journey,
know something of what it means
to be human and weak
and know something about failure.
It speaks to us in the context
of spirit-filled living
and of the daily struggle.
It speaks to every man who will hear it,
saint or sinner,
and says something about the quality of life
within the community of believers.
Now, what is that quality of life?

You see, the life that Jesus brings
is the life of the God who is light.
In Him is no darkness at all
but what
about us?
Caught as we are in our humanness,
our prejudices and weaknesses,
our failures and our moods,
with all the contingencies of our lives
in a fallen world—
what about us?

What about you and I—
   the people who are a part of the dark world
                  into which Jesus came?
        His life has gathered us into a fellowship.
      And I have come to believe with all my heart
      that the passage says,
      that in that fellowship
         we are to live in openness
             and honesty
             and confession
in full and continual awareness
   of the realities of our humanness
     and our weaknesses
     and our failures.
Each of the "if we says" is in some way
        a denying
      or a defending
      or a pretending about our
         real situation
             as
          fallen
          humans.
I'm not saying that the Christian life
  is a perpetual series of failures and guilts
    because that's not true.
But I am reminding us
    that we are human
    and we are weak.
             We are not strong
        we are the have-nots
     and our salvation is by grace.
And all through our journey
  we know the meaning of moods
    and loss of psychic energy.
We know the meaning of failure
and we know the tragedy of broken homes
            and broken relationships
             which we have both received
  and to which we have made our small contribution.

We have been hurt,
            and we have hurt;
                    we have been the "tragic-tee,"
            and we have been the "tragic-tor."
We live in a world of broken relationships
        in which we have shared and
        to which we have contributed.
If we are going to talk about fellowship
                        one with another in Him
and the fact that God has created us
                    in the vast complexities
                    of the interpersonal world
then we can't withdraw ourselves
        and have life with God
        and not pick up our share

                    of both the reality
                    and the fallenness
                of those relationships.
                    We can't do that.

If we start
        the defining, ignoring business
we find ourselves
    moving into darkness
        and lying
            and deceit
            and the light of God
        casts its inevitable judgment
        on our weakness and
            guilt and
            failure.

Well, so far
    we have gathered up
        three fundamental truths:

                    God is light
                we are not light
            and we can't define,
                    defend,
                    pretend,
                or ignore it.

Then how are we going to handle our situation?
Let's look up at the big sign.
Well, thank God, there are three more "if's"
up there to give us hope.
Look at the second line
of each of the three couplets.
If we say . . . NO!

But
if we walk
in the light,
as He is in the light
we have fellowship with one another
and the blood of Jesus, His Son cleanses us from
all sin.
(1 John 1:7)

What does it mean to walk in the light?
If God is light
means God shines—
for me to walk in the light
means for me to walk
in the shining of God.
The best way I know to think about that is
God shines in Jesus
and when I am walking in the light
I am walking with the roof of my life
open to the shining of God.
I understand that kind of mental image—
to walk in the light
means to take the roof off,
open up the ceiling
and let the Son shine in.
Now that is the opposite of
defining
hiding
pretending,
those are the covers—
to walk in the light is to take the covers off.
It means exposing my life
to the verdict of God.

It means all the doors of my life
                    are open to him—
        all the closets
        all the rooms
        and all the cupboards.

And the next "if" clause
    is very much like the first one.
If we say . . . NO!
                        But if we confess our sins,
                            He is faithful and just
                            and will forgive our sins
                        and cleanse us from all unrighteousness.
                                    (1 John 1:9)
I believe that confession
        and walking in the light
            are Siamese twins.
They belong together in the same way
    that the "if we say" clauses
        belong together.
                        Walking in the light means
                            living in openness and confession.
We've got to let God render verdict
        on the whole—
bringing the whole of life into the presence of God
        so that His light shines
                on every part of it.
What a blessed and awesome thing!
                        I think we ought to put in
                        this marvelous parenthesis:
we must all come under the judgment of God,
                but the judgment of God
                    is such that it is our salvation.

I'm thinking of judgment in the sense
        of letting God render verdict,
        of exposure to the truth of God.
Our salvation is not in deceit
                or cover-up
                or hiddenness of our real situation.

It is in the truth
    of the God
        who is light.
The light that reveals
    is the light that cleanses and heals—
        like opening up
          the wounds of our life
        to the sunshine of God's love.
The opening of life to God,
      to His judgment,
      that is where
        we are saved.

That is why we don't get very far
      defining and explaining
      our attitudes and behaviors.
"That wasn't really worry—
    that was concern."   *Beautiful.*
"That wasn't anger—
    that was righteous indignation."   *Lovely.*
"That wasn't a lustful look—
    that was an appreciative glance." *Marvelous.*
You see, I know some of these phrases myself.
    We have got to say "OK, Lord.
        Here it is.
        You name it."
What is so awful in the covering up is that
      we go on,
      unjudged
     unrebuked
    unchecked
    and uncleansed.
What I cover up
    I'm left with—
what I open up
    receives not only the revealing of God,
        but also the healing of God.

And that is the growing edge of life
    what He reveals—
        He heals,
    what He illumines—
        He cleanses
                and that is our salvation.
    God's marvelous grace
    meets us right where we are.
If we confess,
He is faithful,
    He is just,
        He will forgive and cleanse.

The word confession is a beautiful word—
                it really means
            "to say the same."
      It means
    "I say what is."
    It is like the old phrase
              "to own up."
          To confess to something is to own it.
      To own up-have you heard that phrase?
What does that mean—
      it means to go ahead and say,
        "That belongs to me."

Maybe this doesn't happen at your house
        but at our house
        my young son will say,
"Can I take my plate
    and go in
        and watch TV?"
So he puts the food in the plate
    then puts the glass on
    then the silverware
        and the napkin
    and starts into the hall
        balancing all of this precariously.

Sure enough,
    halfway down the hall,
        there is this awful crash.
                "What happened?"
                "It fell."
Now my wife has a thing
    about telling the truth.
She always responds "It what?"
            "It fell."
      "All by itself?"
      "No, I did it."
And this happens, too, at my house,
    the family is seated at the table
        and suddenly a glass of milk goes over.
Everyone jumps up and does something
    but the one who spilled it—
        suddenly he is just paralyzed
           "What happened?"
           "It fell."
And the little bit of perversity in Mary Jo says,
      "It what?"
      "It fell."
"Oh, it did, did it?
    What happened?"
        "I knocked it over."
        "Oh."
I really think this is very important
    and not playing with words at all.

    Somebody runs off with somebody
        and a home splits up.
                What happened?
            It was just one of those things—
"Oh, it was, was it?" It just happened—
"Oh, it did, did it?"
Confession says, "I did it"—
    it is the owning of it.
        But you know, this point of owning it
        is the point of the forgiveness of it.

The good news of it is this—
                    that God in Jesus Christ forgives all sin—
      tangled-messed up relationships,
    .   old destructive habit patterns,
            bitterness and resentment.

Let me push this
            in one more direction.
This passage has helped me in my pilgrimage
            to the point that I have made up my mind
            to never go back
                    and start over again in the Christian life.

It has helped me understand
            that God's intention for me is
                        to keep going on
                        and not start over
                        at every point of failure.
The point of failure should become
                the occasion for immediate confession
                and trust in the forgiveness
                            and cleansing of God.
And it has meant everything for me
                    to make up my mind to that.

My daughter, Susan,
plays the piano beautifully—
    though, I must say, not as beautifully as she should
            in the light of all the lessons we have paid for.
When she would get a new piece when she was younger
she would sit down and begin work on it.
She would make it through the first staff
            and about halfway through the second
            and make a mistake.
You already know the next step.
        She would go back and start over—
                            louder,
make the same mistake
    at the same place
                and do it again—
                        LOUDER!

I've thought a lot about that
  and that's what we do in the Christian life, isn't it?
On the average
    most folk I know have started over
      at least twenty-five times before—
                        probably you have, too.
Well, what are you
going to do now?
Do we need to sing "Just As I Am" thirteen times
              or "Almost Persuaded" fourteen times?
I'm not writing about these precious songs
    that the Holy Spirit
        has used in beautiful ways—
I'm writing about
what I believe to be
God's thing for me
            at my point of failure.
I don't need a new
        and louder beginning
            of the Christian commitment.
        I need to open it up
          and let the light shine,
          and then keep going on.
I already know the first five bars
                of the Christian life
                    by heart.
        God knows I have played them enough.
        I've made up my mind to finish the song.
I probably couldn't do a perfect performance
            if I did it a hundred times—
    and neither can you.
But whether it is a sin,
        or a blunder,
        or a mistake,
        or a failure,
it has to be handled in the same sort of way—
by opening it up to God
        and walking in the light.

There is one more "if" clause.
It begins with a clear statement
 of the divine ideal:
 My little children

   I am writing this to you
  so that you may not sin.
    (I John 2:1)

I understand that, don't you?
  I know what God's intention is—
   I know what is His will
  and I know what is the ultimate goal.
It is life without failure and
 life without sin.
And it is His promise
 that someday we shall be like Him
 for we shall see Him
   as He is.
   (I John 5:2)
But life now is in-between the times—
   between the first coming
   and the second coming—
and we are caught
 here in life between—
   between what we were
   and what we want
    to be.
We know something of the forgiving
    cleansing grace of God
and we know something of what it means
    to be human
    and fallen,
    and weak,
    and failing.
How beautiful that this last "if" clause
 meets us with such profound
    and tender understanding
   of the flow of our lives in Christ.
    His intention is clear.

My little children I am writing this to you
that you sin not . . . but if!
But if anyone does sin
                    we have an advocate with the Father
                    Jesus Christ, the Righteous.
We would never have had the courage
        to put that in yet how desperately we need it.
                            Isn't that great?
                            Let's just put it this way:
My little children
my intention is
                that all marriages be happy
                            and mature
                            and fulfilling—
                                            but if . . .

My little children
I'm writing this
                that all of you be healthy and whole
                        in body and mind—
                            but if . . .

I'm writing this
                so there won't be brokenness,
                            tragedies,
                            scars
                but if . . .
Suddenly into the realities of a fallen world
        and into the brokenness of it comes this healing word:
                we have an advocate.
Not at the point of our achievement,
but at the point of our failure.
            Christ the Advocate is by our side,
                        on our side.
            Righteous Jesus Christ
            and He is the expiation for our sins—
not our struggles
        not our self-hate
                not our self-loathing
                    nor our rash promises or vows—
He is our advocate, our way to handle our sins.

Let's pray together:
Lord Jesus
        teach us to know
                that the quality of life
                    we are to share—
is one of openness and honesty and confession.
Teach us to know
            the answer to our failures.
            Some of us need to know
                            that the answer to deep
                                    guilt and sin
                            is not to define
                                    or defend
                                    or to pretend
but it is to walk in the light.
        It is to take the roof off to Thee.
It is to confess
        to own
        to open up
in the full assurance that the grace of God
                            heals
                        and forgives
                            and cleanses
                    and restores
                        and renews
                    and that Thou does come to stand
                        by our side
                at the point of our failure.
Teach us to live in openness to Thee.
                                        Amen.

Chapter Four

WHAT DOES IT MEAN TO LOVE

Put it down brother; Splangknalevel dialogue;
Love that behaves like Jesus; On becoming a
people people.

Now here is what I have been saying—
you can tell I've been teaching long enough
                            that I "loves" review—
              Jesus brings to us
                    into our world,
                        all the way into our world,
                              the very life of God.
              And the life He brings is a shared life—
              and it always creates a community.
          It isn't Jesus and me,
          it is Jesus and we.
    We really do need each other.
    God has made us this way.
    The quality of life
        within this fellowship of those
        who share the life of Jesus
          is to be one of openness
                    and confession
                    and honesty before Him.

    You see,
    Jesus brings the life of the God
                        who is light.
              This life we share
                  is to express itself outward
                          in the community of believers
                          in terms of love.
                I want to talk about that love.

Read the Word with me.

For this is the message
   which we have heard from the beginning
      that we should love one another,
                              and not be like Cain,
   who was of the evil one and murdered his brother.
                  And why did he murder him?
            Because his own deeds were evil
               and his brother's righteous.
               Do not wonder, brethren,
                  that the world hates you;
   we know that we have passed out of death into life,
      because we love the brethren.
         He who does not love remains in death.
(Pretty strong words, aren't they?)
Anyone who hates his brother is a murderer.
I think he is saying,
      now there are Cain and Abel,
         but let's not talk Cain and Abel,
            let's talk you and me.
         Anyone who hates his brother is a murderer.
            And you know that no murderer
               has eternal life abiding in him.
By this we know love
   that He laid down His life for us,
      and we ought to lay down our lives
         for the brethren.
                        (1 John 3:11-18)

                  What does it mean to love?
                  Let's take a look.
First of all,
let me share with you
      a couple of words and phrases
         that have come to have real meaning for me.

One of them is the phrase "lay down."
I have had problems with these two words.
   It's easy to understand the
                "he laid down his
                life for me" part
                and that's good, that's okay.
But when it comes to the
                "we ought to lay
                    down our lives" part
                  that doesn't go too good.
            I mean I love you—
                  but I don't want to die for you—
                  not before Monday anyway.
And I don't think you want to die for me
  and I'm not sure it would help a whole lot
    even if you did.
  And neither do I think we can explain it by saying
    we must be willing to.
              In fact,
              as we get older
the things we are willing to die for get fewer
                    and fewer.
    The young can die for all causes.
  But the things I'd die for are very few
and the people I would die for are nearly none at all.
You understand that too,
  because that's true of you as well.
But I have been both helped and challenged by this—
    the word "lay down" means precisely what it says.
I know that in the laying down of His life
    He did in fact give His life.
        But before He died, Jesus "laid down His life."
      The word, "lay down"
        comes from the Greek word which means
              "to place" or "to put."
            It means
            just put it down,
            lay it down.

Now He just put His life down for us;
we ought to put our lives down for the brethren.
Thankfully that does not mean go out and die,
    but it does mean go ahead and just put it down.
I'm not sure what all that means,
        but I think I know a little bit about what it means
                                        to hold it back
                                        And that helps—
                                        and hurts.
Sometimes I wonder what are we saving ourselves for.
Now I don't like this anymore than you do,
    it's just that I happen to believe
            that the Bible means what it says
                    . about some of these things
                        even though we don't like them.
        I'm thinking of a man
                                who all his life long saved
                                        and saved
                                        and saved
                                        and held back—
                                            you know—
                        don't loan and don't borrow
                all it brings is trouble and sorrow.
That's the life slogan—don't loan, save, take care—
and all of his life he worked and saved and I guess
                                        he made it.
And do you know what he did when he was about sixty-
                                        four?
                    Yeah-he up and died—
                    that's what he did.
                    And all of the saving,
                    keeping, holding, making
                    making, keeping, holding
                    saving of his life—
                    was down the tubes
                    forever.
    Now I'm not talking about economics.
I'm talking about a lifestyle
    that seeks to preserve, save, keep-for what!!

I hate to tell you this, but I found out over in the
Computer Science Department
that according to the latest statistics the death average is
one hundred percent.
And you know, we are going to die,
we're just going to die.
I thought I'd leave you with that cheerful word—
we're just gonna die.

You know, we want to
save ourselves
and keep ourselves
and hold ourselves back
as though the highest goal in life would be to look good
in our caskets.
It's no special blessing to come to the end of life with
love unshared
selves ungiven
activities unactivated
deeds undone
emotions unextended.
It's not an encouraging thought—
especially at my age in life—
but I have the feeling that when
a person is middle-aged
he ought to be about half used-up.
And when I read this passage
I keep asking myself this question—
what am I saving myself for?
Isn't it God's intention that when we come to the end
of the line
we're just about used up?
Sometime between now and then
we might as well be letting the candle burn
for the light
for the heat
for the warmth and sharing.
As long as we are going to live
and then die
we'd just better live for Jesus
and love and go ahead and let ourselves be used up.

I think I need that at school.
                    A good friend of mine said,
"Teaching is a marvelous profession
                    if it weren't for the students."
About halfway through the fall quarter
        it might be good if you call me up
and remind me
of what I have written to you.

                                But I need to know—
                what am I saving myself for?
                He laid down his life for us—
                    we ought to lay down our lives
                            for the brethren.
As long as I can read that verse
    and say I'd be willing to die if I have to,
            I can go my way untouched
                    and unrebuked.
But when it says to me
            put it down brother—
            put your life down—
            then that meets me day by day
                    and challenges me
                        to decision and
                            discipleship.
And I think that is what the Holy Spirit
            has in mind for me and you.

The second word is just fantastic.
It is the Greek word that is translated "heart"
    and I have to write about it.
        It is not the word "kardia"
            from which we get words like cardiac.
                That is the normal Greek word for heart.
                    The word here doesn't mean heart at all.
                    It is "splangkna".
Isn't that a good word—
                your "splangknas".

See—   "if anyone has the world's goods
                and sees his brother in need
        yet closes his splangknas against him
                how does God's
                        love abide in
                                him?

It's really interesting that the translators must have been
                feeling very civilized
                        at the time this was translated
because what it really means
        is "innards."
    There is a real neat short word for it
            that I hate to use in public.
Have you heard of "splangkna level" dialogue?
Maybe New Testament people didn't know too much
about physiology
    but they sure did know a lot about people
                            and where you feel it
                                when you feel it.
When you have had your feelings hurt
                where does it hurt?
And when you are heavy-hearted
                where does the weight
                            rest?
Not in your heart,
    but in your "splangknas"—that's where.
When there is tension and misunderstanding
                    in your home or at work
where does the dull heaviness rest?
                In your innards—that's where.

                    Now here is the awesome
                and wonderful thing about all this.

If we see our brother in need, yet close up our insides
against him—
if it doesn't get to us
if we keep aloof and cool
and untouched and uninvolved
if it doesn't get to us to tear up
our indigestion
at all—
if we don't
feel it
where we really feel things—
then-listen to this now—
how does God's love abide in us?
Is St. John saying that the love of God is to be identified
with the kind of love that we feel in our innards?
Yes, he's saying that
if you don't feel it there
then how does God's love abide in you?
Does that say anything to us
about the way God loves?
It says to us that God has
opened up his insides to us.
He has revealed His heart
to us
in Jesus Christ.
He is not impassive
and aloof
and untouched
and uninvolved.
He has entered into the realities of our human lives at
the feeling level.
He has exposed himself
and become utterly vulnerable—
hanging out on a cross.
Then let's not love in word, but in truth.
I think this is what John means when he says—
He laid down his life for us;
and we ought to lay down our lives
for the brethren.

I think we need to back away from these verses
    and look at them in a more general way.
                If we are to lay down our lives
                and not hold them back—
                if we are to love . . .
                in deed and truth—
    we need to know what kind of love it is
                He lays on us.
                                What directions
                                does this love take?
                    How are we going to
                    work it out in practice?
I need to tell you,
        if you don't know by now,
        that I have a tendency to exaggerate
                                when I'm enthused.
    And I am wanting to share with you some insights,
two or three things
    that have indeed been life-changing
        for me
            in terms of what this love means.
And though I've talked about them
                and thought about them to some degree
                    I haven't got them all integrated in yet,
so that if I were talking to you instead of writing
                    I'd probably yell once in awhile.

    The first one is this:
in the teaching of First John
    the love of which he speaks
        is not so much directed toward God
                        as toward the brethren.
        Let me give you a couple of scriptures.
He laid down his life for us
    we ought to lay down our lives for the brethren.
                            (I John 3:16)

Herein is love,
  not that we loved God
  but that he loved us
    and sent His Son to be the expiation for your sins.
                Beloved, if God so loved us
                  we ought also
                  to love one another.
                  (I John 4:10,11)

    Now you know,
    when you lay it out like that
    it is as clear as it can be
        but I cannot get over the fact
          of how revolutionary
            and radical
              that is.
          I think most of my life I was fetched up
                    one way or another
              in the idea that we ought to love God;
                      which,
                        as you know,
                          is true.
Let me tell you the first testimony you ever gave.
  Remember the very first testimony you ever gave?
                  "I love the Lord
                  and I want to go
                  all the way with
                      Him."
Where do you suppose that comes from?
      I don't know.
      But by now,
          I guess it is universal.
                  "I love the Lord
                  and I want to go
                  all the way with
                      Him."
And what I am seeing in First John is this—
    God is not so concerned that I love Him
      as that I believe He loves me
        and I love you.

You see we can get in a cycle here
                    God loves me
                                        and I love God
                    and He loves me
                                        and I love Him.
                    "Oh Lord I love thee,
                                        I want to love Thee more,
                                        more love to thee, O
                                        Christ."
He laid down His life for me and so we sing,
                            "I'll live for Him who died for me."
        And it is possible to get this
            into a kind of cocoon
                that withdraws us from the world
                            and from persons
                    in order to love God—
                                    and that's not good.
                I don't want to testify too much here
                but I have to testify a little I suppose
            because what I'm saying comes out of my life
                    and the Word as it has been meeting life.
But I remember—
        I don't quite know how to say this
                        or if I ought to—
        a long time ago
    before I came to school
        I had a lot more time to pray
                            and read the Bible
                                than I do now.
                    That may or may not be true,
                        but that's what I think.
There have been times in my life
    when I spent more time alone
                    in solitude
                        and I prayed more than I do now.
Because when I moved to the college to teach—
    and started teaching Greek every morning at 7:30
                    I mean I entered a whole new world.

And I found two things
  and it took awhile to get them together.
    I found I didn't have hardly any time at all
                        to myself.

But I discovered that as
  I began to love people
    and to care for people
and become involved with people
  I had more joy
        more life
          more tears
            more laughter
            more meaning
  and far greater fun and joy
    than I ever had before.
    Now don't misunderstand that,
I'm not saying we are not to get alone—
      we are.
But I don't think we are to withdraw
      and to say
          "O God I want to love Thee
              do I love Thee
              Lord I love Thee
              let me count the ways."
I think I'm beginning to believe
  that God is not as sentimental
    as we sometimes think He is.
I have weird mental images—
  there are some people
    in some churches that I remember
          and I remember one
        dear, poor, pitiful sister
          who used to stand up
      and say in a slow, whiny way,
        "Well, I love the Lord."
  And I could just see the Lord
    looking down and saying,
        "Oh, I'm so glad."

Do you think God has some giant, heavenly daisy,
and He is saying
"He loves me
he loves me not
he loves me
he loves me not."
You should have been brought up in
the church that I was brought up in—
one of the blessings of it was
that every odd character that ever lived
had a prototype in that church
and I haven't met any strangers
since.
And I can remember a dear sister
who used to get up and talk about
"Oh . . . I love the Lord."
She had her children all spread out on each side of her.
She'd sit back down and one of them would wiggle . .
"Ker-whump!"
You know . . .
"Mommy, can I . . ."
"Ker-whump!"
"I love the Lord . . ."
"Ker-whump!"
Well okay-
and you know I am exaggerating,
but not too much.
It isn't God loves me and
"Lord I need to love Thee more, yes
help me to love Thee more,
I do love Thee,
please help me to love Thee more.
Do I love Thee Lord,
yes, Lord I do love Thee."
He laid down his life for us
and we ought to lay down our lives for the brethren.
Beloved, if God so loved us
we ought also to love one another.

Now how about that?
That means that the flow of the love of God
  is not to be back toward Him—
                        well, please understand;
                        that doesn't sound right,
                        but you know what I mean—
    but love is to be out toward the brother.
Now maybe this is one of those radical things,
                the continuity-discontinuity themes,
  in which this love for the brother
  is in fact, the thing which saves
                        and preserves
                        and expresses
                                our love for God.
        It is in fact,
            in the love for my brother
        that the love of God
            is guaranteed and perpetuated.
And it saves us from sentimentalism
                and egotism
            and self-centeredness
                        in all our holy ways
                        and words
                        and keeps us honest
                                and open
                                and real.
When you come right down to it,
    how do I love God?
  What do I have to give Him that He needs?
                        You know—
                like Paul said in Romans—
"Who has given a gift to Him
  that he might be repaid?"
    For from Him
    and through Him
    and to Him are all things. (Romans 11:35,36)

How can I love Him?
Maybe the only way
that I can love God is by loving you.

Now if that is true
that casts a whole new dimension
on our living relationships with each other.
And I have to say this
that since I have had the privilege
of living among the young
and the Bible study groups
and the fellowships
and the times of talking and sharing
and laughing and crying
and the impositions and the ecstasies—
you know,
the whole thing
that involves you
when you become a "people-people"—
as I have sought to express my trust in God's love for
me
by deliberately
consciously loving persons—
I think I love God more
and better
and happier
than I ever did.
And it doesn't come by withdrawing—
don't forget what we have been saying—
God has cast us into the world
of the intricacies of inter-personal relationships
and all this thing does hang together.
You see,
God is Trinity—Father, Son, Spirit.
The dynamics of the inner life of God
is the dynamics of giving
and receiving
and loving.

Some have said that the Holy Spirit is the bond of love
                              between the Father and Son
                                    and the bond of love
                    that reaches out to include all mankind
                              in that Holy fellowship;
so that our sharing of the experience of God in the power
of His Spirit is,
                  in fact,
an extension of the dynamic of love within God himself.
And the love of which He speaks
                              is not so much toward God
                                    as toward the brother.
That is quite radical really,
                  and I think we'll all continue to say
                              "I love the Lord."
All right, but don't talk about loving the Lord
                        and not loving our brother—
      somehow they go together
        they belong together
                              you cannot separate them.
In fact,
      "If a man loves God and hates his brother . . ."
                                    that is,
      if he says he loves God and hates his brother,
                              the Bible says
                                    he's a liar.
                        That's pretty strong.
I really need to believe that God
    is not so much concerned that I emote toward Him
        as that I act in love toward you
        and believe that He loves me.
I think that God is more concerned that I believe He
                                    loves me
                        than that I love Him.
            And that I express that trust in His love
                        by deliberately,
                        consciously
                  loving my brother.

And don't forget
        that "brother" means fellow Christian.
                    Of course, we are to love
        all those who come into the circle of our world,
        but the place where love is to be going on
        is in the community of believers who share
        in the life of Christ.
If love is not going on between us who know the Lord,
                        what good is talk about loving people
                                            "out there?"
                It doesn't mean anything anywhere
                if it doesn't mean anything here between us
                                        in the fellowship.
The Spirit won't let us generalize this too much.
                        John is not talking about
                        a spirit of good will
                        toward mankind.
                He means love to real live people
        beginning with our Christian brothers and sisters
right here in the fellowship.

Here is another insight
                that has been changing me.
                It has come
                from hearing John say—
"When you say love think Jesus."
        It is not enough to say "God is love."
        The Bible doesn't end there.
You can take that statement by itself
        and make it a foundation stone—
            on which you can build
        just about any kind of religion you want.
        Christian Science is built on the idea "God is love."
            Buddhism
                Hinduism
                    Universalism
                        Humanitarianism
                            can all be built on
                                    "God is love."

That's not a Christian statement standing alone.
Here's the Christian statement—
"God so loved the world He sent His Son
so that we might live through Him."
When the Bible says "God is love,"
it does not mean
God has a general benevolent feeling
toward mankind
and has opened many roads
toward which we may struggle to find Him.
It means that God has given Himself to us
in Jesus Christ.
The defining act
of the love of God is the coming of Jesus.
The word love needs a definition, doesn't it?
Jesus is the "lived out" word.
I read a beautiful thing once,
I wish I'd thought it myself.
I love to get good quotes
and never put down where I got them
until pretty soon
I think I thought them up
myself.
"The word love, needs a dictionary
and for Christians the dictionary is Jesus Christ.
He took that chameleon of a word
and gave it a fast color
so that ever since
it has lustered with His life and
teaching—
dyed in the crimson of Calvary
and shot through with the glories of
Easter morning."
Isn't that great?
That should be in the Bible
some scribe just missed it.

When we say love
    we can mean anything.
There are big words in Greek for love—
              "eros"
              "philos"
              "agape."
Eros is the love of desire—
        love of not only sex and lust—
    but love that seeks to own, to possess, to have.
A man says, "I just love oranges."
    If the orange could speak,
                it would say, "You don't love me—
                    you just want to squeeze me!"
I love paintings
I love antiques
    or music
    or books—
    which mostly means I want to have them.
There's another level—philos,
from which we get words like
              Philadelphia—the city of brotherly love
    and fellowship.
    We have in common
      we give
        we receive
        we share.
                  This is beautiful love
            and is God's precious gift to us
        but this is not the love
            that John is talking about.
        He is talking about
        love that thinks Jesus in the loving.
Agape love—
        which is not simply giving love,
            but giving love
            in the context of God's sending
                his son.

Now,
I don't want to run this in the ground
but
when you say love, think Jesus.
That's the Christian view.

By love
we do mean more
than a benevolent spirit toward mankind.
That makes me
think of another
good quote I
read somewhere.
"It's a shame that in the minds
of so many, the Christian
religion has been identified
with pious ethical behavior
together with a vague belief
in God suffused with aesthetic
emotionalism and a mild
glow of humanitarian
benevolence."
Isn't that great?
Or perhaps awful.

That makes you think
of a nice pastor
in a nice church
preaching a nice sermon
to a nice congregation
telling them to be nicer—
"the bland leading the bland".
That is not
what the New Testament means by love.
Love is a strong word.
It does not mean total tolerance
or universalism.
It means that when we say love—
we are thinking of Jesus.

We are sharing His love—
                              not mutuality
                              not congeniality
                              not what you have
                              in real neat service clubs
                    plus the inspiration of the Holy Spirit
                              not mutual affection
                              plus blessing.
It expresses itself
   in that love that comes
      from Jesus Christ.

What is it that makes it possible for people to
   have long, enduring
      deepening, close, affectionate
         friendships
      without growing sordid
      without wife-swapping
      without it becoming unclean
                    and adulterated?
I know we have our troubles and every so often
                                        somebody
                           runs off with the wrong
                                        somebody.
But what is it that makes it possible
   for couples
      and families
         and friends
            to love each other
               reach out to each other
                  and touch each other
                              for years
                                   and years
                                   and years
without its becoming unclean or sordid—
                         not denying chemistries
                              or vibrations
                              or potentials,
                         not denying temptations
                              or possibilities?

How can we be friends
for long periods of time
and it still be good
and wholesome
and rich
and beautiful
and supportive?
Because the love of Jesus
strengthens us.
Something very precious happens
when we say in Jesus
"I love you."
His love is always healing, cleansing
lifting, preserving.
It is a good word—
because Jesus gave it a fast color.

Here is another life-changing insight for me
that is both old and new.
Love is commanded.
Some things cannot be commanded
and we think love is one of them.
But right here it says just as plain as day—
And this commandment we have from him
that he who loves God
should love his brother also.
(1 John 4:21)

We are commanded
to love
one another.
You see,
it has to move suddenly
out of the realm of attraction.
There are some people
that we like
and then there are the other kind.
And some who like us
and some we can't understand.

Now look,
if Christian love is restricted to those we have
                                natural, warm feeling for
                    we have limited our world
                        to the little group we happen to be
                                                    around.

        But,
love is commanded
        and if we are going to talk about love
            we have to move out of the level of
                            liking
                            and emotion
                                and feeling
                                    and warmth
                                        to the level of the will—
                                            a posture
                                            a stance
                                                an attitude
                                                a frame of mind
                                    a life's direction toward others
                        that's conditioned by our understanding
                                                    of God's
                                    self-giving in Jesus.
            We are commanded.
            It isn't as though
                        we had any
                            alternative.
            Have we accepted that yet,
                        do you suppose?

I think it is time to get more practical—
    and maybe time for a word of review.
                            We have been saying
                            that the life of God
                        that Jesus brings into our world
                    is a shared life.
                    God's love for us that "comes down"—
                                        the vertical line—
is to be expressed out through the
    horizontal line of our personal relationships.

God's love for us is defined
  by the giving of His Son, Jesus,
and love for each other
  is defined by Him, too.
Our love for each other behaves like Jesus.

Let me try to put some handles
  on all this talk about love
    to help us pull it down
      into the flow of daily life.
  I'm sure that what I'm going to say now
              is in First John somewhere.
            You may have to look
                between the lines
              and in the margins—
              but surely it is there.

Love that behaves like Jesus
      means care for persons
            as persons.
          We are to see persons in a personal way,
                not in a "thingy" way.
  We have a tendency to put people into categories—
            that's "thingy"
            that "thingizes" them—
              it turns them into "its" instead of
                          "yous".
  You know how Southerners are.
  I do 'cause I'm not one.
  You know how Westerners are,
              you know how the Mexicans
                    the Blacks
                  the Orientals are.
              Put them into categories,
            slip them into little slots
                      categorized
                      depersonalized
              massed-up
                and that's not love.
          Love sees the person.

I never will forget one afternoon
    when I was coming back from a retreat
      up in the Sierras.
           I was taking the back way home
and there were
about four or five cars coming down the mountains.
        It was back of Fresno
        out in the hot valley
        and it was about 110°
        and we took a kind of a back road
        and they were doing repair work on it.
And we were just cruising along there and a patrolman
              pulled us over.
Five of us—and it was just dumb.
Here we were 50 miles from nowhere—
    five irate drivers and this young cop.
There we stood in the boiling sun
    mad as could be
        at the injustice of the whole thing.
        And right in the midst
        of all my disgust I
        looked at this young
        patrolman—and he was young—
and he was writing out tickets to five angry drivers
        and he was trembling.
        That was one of my better days.
He was writing with nervous hands
    and the creases of his pants were just shaking.
        And suddenly my whole attitude changed—
not that he was right—
    but it meant my whole relationship to him changed
      because suddenly I saw him as a young policeman
        nervous as could be, wanting to do it right
          and probably wishing to goodness
            he could have let us go.
      But there he was—
        caught
        and trembling
        and nervous
        and suddenly I knew how he felt.

Behind the uniform was a real,
                    live people.
            It's kind of an awesome thing,
                            isn't it?
        Suddenly my own guilts are rising,
we all know those people who fade into the furniture—
                            you know,
                    you don't hear them
                    you don't see them
                you don't know they are there.
        But I've learned a few things the hard way—
                    and one of them is
        that there isn't anybody who is a nobody.
        Everybody is a somebody
                    and
        everybody is a "real live people"—
with real hopes
        and real dreams
            and fears
                and longings
                    and desires.

I've learned a few things about myself lately.
        I'm really very sensitive.
                    It took me a long time to accept that.
But I am—
        I'm sensitive as I can be.
        I think I might make a good pastor
            if there weren't any such things as votes.
            I "loves" them contracts.
                And I can't stand votes—
                    I think they're of the devil.
                But I know I'm sensitive
            and I'm probably half neurotic about it.
And on the heels of that newfound knowledge
    has come another fascinating discovery—
        everybody is sensitive,
            there isn't anybody who's not sensitive.

"Oh you know so and so—you couldn't hurt him.
It runs like water off a duck's back."
              Oh no it doesn't.
              Did you know that—
                        skinny people are sensitive
                        that fat people are sensitive
                    that hairy people are sensitive
                      that bald people are sensitive
                        and tall people are sensitive
              and short people are sensitive?
                        Everybody is sensitive.
                    Love says I care for you
                                        as a person.
Love says in word and response I see you
                              I hear you
                              I know you are there.
          I am aware of *you*—
                              I see *you*
                              I hear *you*
                              I know *you* are there.
That's almost so simple as to be ridiculous.
But nothing has made more impression on me
                        than just that very thing.
I went to a big church convention one time
and it was just like I knew it was going to be.
                                        You know,
                        here's this thingy on you,
and you meet somebody and he looks at your badge
                                        and says,
              "Hi, how are you?"
Then before you can answer
      he's looking over your shoulder
                  for somebody better than you to talk to.
And so you spend a week bumping into people—
              never having time to talk to anybody
              and nobody ever really looks at you.
"Oh, hi, how are you?"
and you're on your way.
I don't know who everybody was looking for
      but everybody was more important than I was.

And then sure as the world,
     some guy you don't especially want to see
     will just glue in on you.
          But love says
               I see you.
                    Just like that—
                    I *see you.*

Here's a little thing—
do you want a handle for all this?
          Love says look at the people you're talking to.
                              Just look at them—
                                   go ahead—
                                   look at them.
                    Don't look up there at the ceiling
                                   don't look over there
                    don't put your hands in your pockets
                              or draw on the ground.
                    Don't kick the tire just look at them.
                                        I see you.
I remember not too long ago—
          not long enough ago—
I was sitting in the living room reading
and my daughter, Susan, said, "Daddy,
                    Daddy—
                         Daddy."
And Mary Jo, her mother, said, "Why don't you,
               just for fun, count up the times
     you have to say "Daddy" before he answers?"
          Now I heard that
               and it didn't bless me a whole lot.
I think the thing that hurt the most was
     that I'm not that kind of person.
You know—I'm the warm,
               friendly,
               caring,
                    outgoing type—
                         I tell people that
                         everywhere I go.

I'm that type of person.
But here I was reading a book—
                    actually it testifies to my
                    fantastic powers of concentration—
and if that day at school was a normal day at school
I had listened
        and talked
        and shared
            with five or six students
and I came home and was sitting in my living room
    reading a book and my very own daughter
        who is very precious to me
            was saying to me, "Daddy,
                    Daddy—
                        Daddy."
                    That's not too good, is it?
Love says
        I'll put the paper down,
        I'll turn the knob off,
        I will look
        and I will listen
        and all of me is present here
                    to listen and
                    to look at you.

When I go home after spending a weekend
                    speaking at a retreat or something,
        if it has been a normal weekend at home—
            you know—I've been gone,
                    I've been wined and dined,
                    I've had some good fellowship,
                    I've had some solitude—
        it's about time for the dishwasher to go out
    or the radiator hose to break
  or the battery to go down
  or some other dumb thing.
Or the favorite trick—that being the bank balance
                    getting all fouled up.

You see,
   I go back home to my wife
   and she has been father,
               mother,
               and mostly chauffeur,
               and life has gone around and around—
and I come back all filled up with what I've been doing
   and she's all filled up with what she's been doing
     and since I'm the one who's talking about love
       guess who ends up listening.
Here's the way it ought to be.
              I'm not testifying just
              telling you how it ought to be.
When I go home, she'll say to me,
     "How did it go?"
And I ought to say,
          "Fantastic. I wish you had been there.
          How did your weekend go?"
And then I need to just be quiet for half an hour or more
                and just listen.
                  You see,
       her words can come into my ears
          while I'm looking around
       waiting to tell her about this and that.
But I need to just lay my words aside and look

                and listen
      and bring all of my attention to her—
               as a person.
Isn't that what love means?
All of me is here—
   at attention
   to care,
     and to will your good.
It is really interesting that half the people
     who come into my office—
         well, more than that but I hate to admit it—
        begin our conversations by saying—
"Now I know you don't have any answers for me"—
        which helps my ego tremendously.

But really what people need from me is not answers—
                    but a real
                        live person
                            listening
                                and caring.
That's what love means—
                I see you
                    I hear you
                            I know you are there.
                    Listen to your husband—
                                look at him.
                    Listen to your wife—
                                look at her.
                    Listen to your children—
                                look at them.
What if we really listened—
what if we really looked—
what if we really saw each other?

When I was a child we lived way out in the country,
    way out in the San Joaquin Valley in central California.
        It was fifteen miles to Delano
            where we went to school
                        and twenty-five miles another way
                        to Porterville,
                            where we went to church
                    and in the other direction
            there wasn't anything
                    but the foothills of the Sierras.
If you came to see us,
    you came to see us—
because nobody ever was just passin' by.
                            We lived so far
                                out in the country
                    that when the Electrolux man came
                        we had him stay for supper.
My father was a quiet man
but I can remember when people would drive
        all the way from town
                just to talk to him.

And I can remember times
when people would come out
and I could hear the feeling and emotion
but not always the words they were
saying to Dad,
and my Dad would be
saying stuff like "Hm-m.
Well, my, my.
Well, isn't that a sight.
Hmph, yes sir."
Then after awhile
the fellow would say—
"Well, Mr. Welch,
I sure do thank you for your help."
And he'd get in his car
and ride the twenty miles back home
and my father had said,
"Hmph, now isn't that a sight."
I'll tell you something—
twenty miles
is not too far to go
to talk to someone who will listen
and care
and look
and understand
and hear
even if all he says is
"Well, what do you know."
That's true, isn't it?
I'm getting guilty
about how little I really listen—
let's talk about
another handle
we can put on love.

Love says I release you
        and will not judge you.
        I'm not sure that writing about this
                will help my guilt any—
                this is a hard one.
I wish I'd written about it when my children were little.
        I could have released them then
    when they were too dependent to be released.
It's much harder now that they are getting independent.
                        But we don't own each other.
                        I don't own my children,
                        I don't own my wife.
Our ultimate ties
        are ties of love
                that must be freely given.
                I am commanded to love
                        but not to own
                                or control
                                or dominate.

        Every once in a while
        I need to engage in a little mental exercise
    that puts my family up on a large pedestal
                        about six feet high.
    I walk around the pedestal and look them over,
                        one by one, and say,
                        "I love you
                        I release you.
                I am responsible to you
                        and for you—
                        but I do not own you.
    I will not force you to find your fulfillment
                        in my fulfillment—
                but I'll let you go
            to be your own person
        and find your own fulfillment
                supported by my love and care."
How easy to write about this exercise
        and how hard to do it.

It is a wonderful experience
  to be with college students—
  to be about the age of their parents
      and not be a parent,
  to be a father figure to some of them
      and not be a father.
Though I'm not really a father figure
    because I'm too young.
I love them
    and care very much about them
    but I do not own them
 and cannot control what they do
nor act as judge over what they do.
    I have no alternative—
    I must release them.
And the marvelous
  happy
  surprising thing is this:
     persons change
     in the atmosphere
     of releasing,
      unjudging love!
I don't mean that it's a refined, Christian way
 of getting people to do what you want them to—
but caring
  releasing
  unjudging love
    deliberately given in the love of Jesus
    becomes the agent for beautiful change
      in a person's life.

   But oh, the spirit of judgment.
Do you know how to be happy with a group of people
      for a long time?
      Don't judge.
  A spirit of judgment will kill the honeymoon.

That's precisely the point
    that brings about the old proverb—
        if you can keep the young
          converts
      away from the old saints
      long enough to get established
      you'll be alright—
  because the old saints have been touched
        with a spirit of cynicism
            and judgment.
Someone new comes into the church
    and says, "Isn't the pastor marvelous"
      and "Isn't the choir fantastic"
      and I can just hear the old saint—
        "Dearie, you just wait around
           awhile—you'll see."
That's true, isn't it?
It's not right
    but it's true.
To the newcomer
    it's just heaven on earth
    in the community,
but let them hang around awhile and our cynicism
          will get them.
        It's catching, isn't it?
        It's the plague.

You would not believe some of the letters
    that students show me from their parents.
    And parents wouldn't believe
      that students show them to me, either.
I read letters that say in all kinds of ways—
      "I don't trust you
        you aren't good
    when will you ever change
  you are always late, why don't you write
      you aren't responsible
      you are a disappointment
after all we've done for you,
    you'll have to get married—
      you'll get pregnant."

I have seen the long arm of parental control
                              and judgment
   reach across the miles from home to dormitory
and almost destroy the precious
                        growing, seeking life
           of a young college student.
If I were speaking in public
  I think I would be yelling about now.
      That deadly spirit of judgment is indeed the plague.
But love,
      Jesus' kind of love,
      has the releasing
              affirming power to stay the plague
                              and heal our lives.
   What a handle—
           I love you
           I release you
           I will not judge you.
We really do need each other.
All this talk about love is not something ethereal
                              and distant.
      It has handles that reach right down to where we are.
Let's pray a moment together.

Lord Jesus, help us to learn to show love.
      Help us to take time to listen
              to give our attention to the ones around us
           to be more aware of the sensitivities of others.
      Help us to see people as people—
      as real live people
           with feelings and concerns
              that are just like ours.
Help us Lord not to judge
   and help us not to allow our cynicism
      to deprive others of joy.
           Teach us Lord, to love
              In deed and in spirit.
              Amen.

Chapter Five

WE REALLY DO NEED EACH OTHER

Let me just tell you this true thing before
        I stop writing.
At school a few years ago
there was a summer school course in "Group and
                                    Interpersonal
                                    Relations."
        About a dozen people took the class
        and at the end of it
            they decided they wanted to do something
                            together
                    as kind of closing to the class.
                    You know,
                    they had come to know each other,
                        and to share each other,
                and really be personal to each other
                        and break down walls
                        and so forth—
so they decided to get together and take a hike
                            up to Hennigar Flats.
Now, Hennigar Flats is about three miles
        up the side of the mountain behind the campus
        and it takes about an hour and a half
            for anyone to make the hike.

So they set the day
        and made the sandwiches
        and made the chocolate
        and brought the cold drinks
        and the back packs
        and they got all gathered up
                for the safari
        and they started up the mountain—
                together.
But it wasn't long until
the strong, stalwart ones were up in front and
  the other ones were back in the middle and
      way back at the end of the line
              was a girl named Jane—
        who was, you might say,
              out of shape.
At the front was Don—
        a big, strong, former paratrooper.
He and some others—the strong ones—
      were up in front and
the weak ones were back in the back and
        way in the back
          was Jane.
           And Don said—
        it was he who told me the story—
     he looked back a couple of switchbacks
           and saw Jane
   and the Lord told him
   that he had just better go back
   and walk with her.
That's kind of hard on him because he has a need to be
          first.
But he went down
   and started walking with Jane
   and the people in the level above called down,
           "Come on up.
           It's great up here."
        And Jane yelled, "I don't think I can
           make it."

And they hollered, "Yeah, you can.
Try harder, come on up."
And every time they called to her
down went her own sense of worth
down went her own sense of value—
"I can't make it."
"Oh, yeah, you can. Come on."

So the strong went on ahead
and the weak hung behind
and here was ,ane
and she never made it to the top.

Now, look what you have.
You have a group—
we know each other
we like each other
we want to do this together
let's go to Hennigar Flats together.
But before long, you have divided
the strong and the weak
the haves and the have-nots
and the ables and the unables.
So what started out as a group
has now become a fragmented collection.
And so the strong say,
"You can do it."
And the weak say,
"No, I can't."
And so the strong say
"Try harder"—
which is a big help.
That's a big help.
And she didn't make it.
Thankfully, that's not the last chapter.
They must have learned their lessons
because they decided that was no way
to end the fellowship of that class
and they got together and decided
to do it again.

But they made some new rules—
                    it was everybody go
                        or nobody go
                and they were all going
                        together.
So they set the day
                and made the sandwiches
                and made the chocolate
                and brought the cold drinks
                and the back packs
                and they got all gathered up
                        for the safari,
                and they started up the mountain.
It took them four hours to make it to the top,
                and the water was all gone
                and the cold drinks were all gone
                and the sandwiches were all gone
                and the chocolate was all gone
                and the back packs were empty
                        but they all made it,
                            together.

Let me share with you
        the thing that this real life parable
            has been saying to me—
            we have got to go together.
Christian fellowship is no place
            for get in or get out—
                it's get in,
                get in.
And if you need to slow down—
                you slow down.
That's why it's good for us to read scripture
            and sing hymns together—
            the slow folks have to speed up
    and the fast folks have to slow down
    and we have to do it together.
                        I know, don't you,
                that it is God's intention
                that we go together as a body.

It doesn't help much for those who have made it
  to say to us weaklings—
        "Try harder.
        See, I've done it,
          so you can make it."
That makes me think of some dear old grandmother
  whose children are all gone,
    who spends all day praying
      and listening to holy records,
saying to a young mother
  going out of her mind
    with little kids and noise—
             "Oh, honey, just get
              alone with God."
             Yeah, thanks a lot.
          You can't even get alone
        in the bathroom anymore.

You know something—
we're all just people who need each other.
We're all learning
  and we've all got a long journey ahead of us.
      We've got to go together
          and if it takes us until Jesus comes
      we better stay together
      we better help each other.
  And I dare say
    that by the time we get there
      all the sandwiches will be gone
    and all the chocolate will be gone
    and all the water will be gone
    and all the backpacks will be empty.
But no matter how long it takes us
      we've got to go together.
      Because that's how it is
         in the body of Christ.

It's all of us
  in love
    in care
      in support
        in mutuality—
          we really do need each other.
          Let's pray.

Oh, Lord Jesus,
  bring us together,
  keep us together

          seeing,

            hearing,

              aware,

                sensitive.
              We need to look at our children
          and listen to our parents
        and be sensitive to each other
      and aware of each other.
          Teach us to know that it's Thy will
            that we go together.
          Teach us to know that it's not
            our mutualities
              and congenialities
                that bind us—
        it's the life of Jesus Christ
          that binds us—
        and so we belong together
              and we must go together.
                        Amen.